THE FACE OF THE EARTH
MOUNTAINS
JENNY VAUGHAN

Editorial planning
Jollands Editions

MACMILLAN
EDUCATION

First published 1987

Published by
MACMILLAN EDUCATION LTD
Houndmills, Basingstoke, Hampshire RG21 2XS
and London
Companies and representatives
throughout the world

Designed and produced by BLA Publishing Limited,
Swan Court, East Grinstead, Sussex, England.

Also in LONDON · HONG KONG · TAIPEI · SINGAPORE · NEW YORK

A Ling Kee Company

Illustrations by Keith Diaper, Chris Rothero/Linden Artists, Brian Watson/Linden Artists, and BLA Publishing Limited
Colour origination by Waterden Reproductions Limited
Printed and bound in Spain by
Gráficas Estella, S. A. Navarra.

British Library Cataloguing in Publication Data

Vaughan, Jennifer
   Mountains. — (The face of the earth)
   — (Macmillan world library)
   1. Mountains — Juvenile literature
   I. Title   II. Series
   551.4'32   GB512

ISBN 0-333-42627-4
ISBN 0-333-42620-7 Series

Acknowledgements
The Publishers wish to thank the following organizations for their invaluable assistance in the preparation of this book.

Canadian High Commission
Swiss National Tourist Office

Photographic credits
t = top b = bottom l = left r = right

cover: Douglas Dickens

4 ZEFA; 5*t* South American Pictures; 5*b* John Waters/ Seaphot; 7*t* J.G. James/Seaphot; 8 Ed Rotberg; 9 The Hutchison Library; 10 Douglas Dickens; 11*t* The Hutchison Library; 11*b* Douglas Dickens; 12, 13 ZEFA; 14 Claudio Galasso/Seaphot; 15 South American Pictures; 16 The Hutchison Library; 17 Franz Camenzind/ Seaphot; 18 R.J. Hart; 18/19 R. & D. Keller/NHPA; 19 Ivor Edmonds/Seaphot; 20 ZEFA; 21 Douglas Dickens; 22 ZEFA; 23, 26 South American Pictures; 27 The Hutchison Library; 28, 29*t* ZEFA; 29*b*, 30 Douglas Dickens; 32, 33*t*, 33*b* ZEFA; 34 Douglas Dickens; 35 Swiss National Tourist Office; 36*t* John Lythgoe/ Seaphot; 36*b* Douglas Dickens; 37, 38 ZEFA; 39 Ardea; 40 ZEFA; 40/41 Swiss National Tourist Office; 41 South American Pictures; 42, 43*t*, 43*b* ZEFA; 44 Ardea; 45*t* Canadian High Commission; 45*b* ZEFA

Note to the reader
In this book there are some words in the text which are printed in **bold** type. This shows that the word is listed in the glossary on page 46. The glossary gives a brief explanation of words which may be new to you.

Contents

Introduction

Mountains and hills are like huge wrinkles in the Earth's surface. They rise higher than the land around them. Mountains are higher than hills. Most mountains are more than 700 m above the land around them. Only about one twentieth of the Earth's surface is made up of mountains. You can see where they are if you look at the map on page 24.

Mountains are usually in long lines called **ranges**. Several ranges next to each other are called **chains**. There are also huge chains of mountains under the sea. Their highest **peaks** make islands.

Wind, rain and snow

The height of a mountain is measured in metres above the level of the sea, or **sea level**. The air becomes thinner as the mountain gets higher. The air cannot hold on to the sun's warmth, so it gets colder. The air is so cold on some high mountains that there is always snow on the ground.

One side of a mountain often has more rain than the other side. The rainy side usually faces the sea. As the wind passes over the sea, it collects drops of moisture. When these clouds of moisture rise to pass over the mountain, rain or snow falls. By the time the wind reaches the other side it is dry. There is little or no rain left to fall.

▼ Mount Everest is the tallest mountain in the world. Its peak is 8848 m above sea level. Everest is part of the Himalayas in Asia.

▶ This boy from Peru and his herd of llamas live high up in the Andes Mountains. They are nearly 4000 m above the sea.

▼ The North American grizzly bear has very thick fur. It can live in the cold mountains of Alaska. It can safely hunt for food over a large area of land.

Staying alive

Many plants and animals live on the lower slopes of mountains. People have farms and grow crops where there is plenty of rain.

Higher up the mountains, the soil is thin, the wind is strong and it is colder. There may be less rain. Farming is hard.

The people and animals there have to find ways of getting food, shelter and warmth. They change or **adapt** to the conditions in which they live. Their hearts and lungs grow larger to help them get enough **oxygen** from the thinner air. Oxygen is the part of the air that we need to breathe.

People often visit the mountains to enjoy mountain sports, like walking, climbing and skiing.

Many plants and animals cannot **survive** on farmland or near people's homes. They can only find safety among the mountains.

Making mountains

The Earth is about 4600 million years old. The Himalayas are only 50 million years old. The dinosaurs were already **extinct** when the Himalayas were made.

The tallest mountains are usually the newest. Older mountains have been worn down over the years by wind, rain and ice.

Inside the Earth

The centre of the Earth is called the **core**. It is made up of the inner core and the outer core. The core is surrounded by a 2900 km layer of heavy rock, called the **mantle**. Some of the mantle is not solid but liquid. This is the **magma**.

The outside layer of the mantle is the **crust**. The crust is no more than 70 km thick. The crust is made up of large sections called **plates**. Over millions of years, the plates drift into new positions. As they do so the shape and position of the Earth's **continents** change. Mountains are made when these plates move together and **collide**.

Making the largest mountains

The huge collisions between the plates of the Earth's crust happen very slowly. The ocean floor between two continents can be pushed upwards in great folds. We call mountains that are made in this way **fold mountains**.

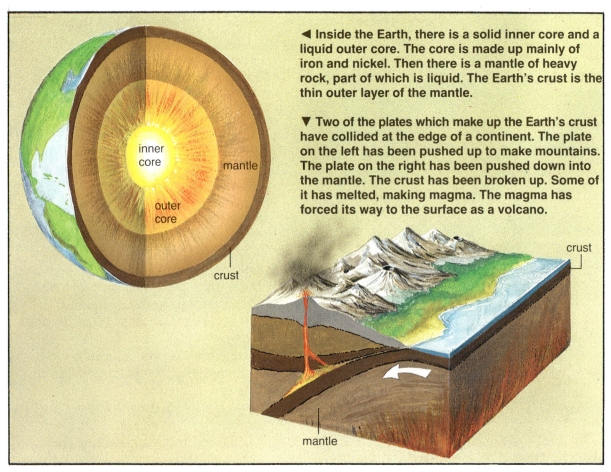

◄ Inside the Earth, there is a solid inner core and a liquid outer core. The core is made up mainly of iron and nickel. Then there is a mantle of heavy rock, part of which is liquid. The Earth's crust is the thin outer layer of the mantle.

▼ Two of the plates which make up the Earth's crust have collided at the edge of a continent. The plate on the left has been pushed up to make mountains. The plate on the right has been pushed down into the mantle. The crust has been broken up. Some of it has melted, making magma. The magma has forced its way to the surface as a volcano.

The Himalayas are fold mountains. The plate carrying India collided with the rest of Asia, pushed up the ocean floor and made the Himalayas. Scientists have found rocks high in the Himalayas which contain the remains, or **fossils**, of sea animals. These rocks once lay on the ocean floor.

The Rocky Mountains of North America and the Andes of South America are also fold mountains. They were made in a different way. When the plates collided, one plate was forced down into the Earth's mantle. The other plate was forced upwards into the mountains. Mountains made in this way are usually found at the edges of continents, close to the sea.

Fold mountains are some of the highest of the world's mountain ranges. They include the Alps, the Carpathians and the Pyrenees of Europe and the Urals of the USSR. The Great Dividing Range of Australia is a very old range of fold mountains. They have been worn away by wind and weather. When they were first made they were much higher.

Block mountains

Where the crust of the Earth is weak, cracks or **faults** are made. Sometimes parts of the crust sink, leaving the other parts standing high above them. At other times, parts of the Earth's crust are pushed upwards.

Mountains made like this are called **block mountains**, because they are made up of blocks of the Earth's crust. The Sierra Nevada in California is a range of block mountains. Its highest peak is Mount Whitney. It is 4418 m above sea level.

The Ruwenzori Range in Uganda in East Africa is made of block mountains. The highest peaks are more than 5000 m above sea level. There is snow on the peaks. The name 'Ruwenzori' means 'the rain maker'. This is because, like all mountains, the Ruwenzori affect the weather around them.

▲ You can see the folds of rock in this cliff on the English coast. Once these layers of rock were straight. Then they were pushed together until they folded and moved upwards.

▼ Block mountains are made when land is pushed up between cracks, or faults, in the Earth's surface. They are also made when a part of the land sinks leaving the other part above it.

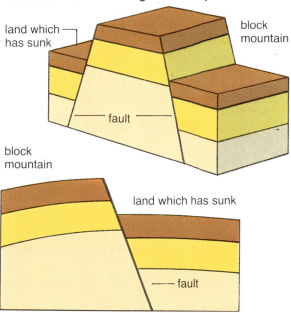

land which has sunk

block mountain

fault

block mountain

land which has sunk

fault

Weather, water and wind

▼ Ayers Rock in Australia is made of sandstone. It is all that is left of a large mountain that has been worn away, or eroded, over thousands of years.

Australia's Great Dividing Range has been worn away by wind and weather. This happens to all mountains.

Ice, rain and the heat of the sun start to break up the rocks that make up a mountain. This is called **weathering**. The softer rocks are broken up first, leaving the harder peaks. Then the rocks are carried away by wind, water and ice. This is called **erosion**. Over millions of years the highest mountains can be worn down by the wind and weather to the same height as the land around them.

Rocks under attack

Weathering happens in several ways. Rain and melting snow play the biggest part. Water washes away soil and soft rock. The water also **dissolves** some kinds of rock by eating into them and making deep cracks.

Heat from the sun warms the rocks during the day. This makes them swell, or **expand**. At night the rocks cool and shrink. This can make them crack. Water gets into the rock through the cracks. If the water freezes, it turns into ice which pushes the rocks outwards. The wind blows stones and sand against the rock and wears it away. All these actions break up the rock.

Now erosion begins to work. Broken rock falls down the mountain side. Rain, snow and ice help to carry it down. The piles of rock pieces are called **scree**.

Running water

Water plays the largest part in erosion. Water may be melted snow or ice or it may be rain. As the water drains off the mountain side, it finds the easiest route. The water collects together in streams and runs down towards the valley below.

Mountain streams are small but fast. They carry pieces of rock and sand with them. These pieces help to wear into the rocks. Softer rock is worn away. The stream cuts into the mountain, making a V-shaped valley. Sometimes it reaches hard rock which it cannot cut through. It pours over this as a waterfall. The waterfall gets higher as more soft rock is worn away at the bottom of the waterfall.

On the way down the mountain, several streams may join and flow together. By the time the water reaches the lower land it may be travelling along only a few channels. These large streams will join and flow on as a much bigger river. The land gets flatter and the river slows down. It drops some of the soil and stones it has been carrying.

The journey to the sea

As the river flows towards the sea, it may be joined by other rivers. Each may have come from a different area of high land. Together, these rivers make up a **drainage system** for a large area.

The Mississippi River starts from Lake Itasca in northern Minnesota, near the Great Lakes. It is joined by the Missouri which flows from the Rocky Mountains. It is also joined by the Ohio which starts in the Appalachian Mountains. The river reaches the sea near New Orleans. It carries about 500 million tonnes of mud and sand to the sea each year. Much of this is dropped at the river mouth making a marshy plain. The river channels its way through the mud and sand in a fan shape. This region of channels is called a **delta**.

Over millions of years the mud and sand from rivers hardens into rock on the ocean floor. This may be lifted up to become part of a mountain once again.

▼ This stream is high up in the mountains of Pakistan. It flows fast and carries pieces of rock and sand. Over thousands of years, the stream has cut deep into the rocks of the mountain. The stream has made a steep-sided valley. You can see that the valley is shaped like a V.

Rivers of ice

Glaciers are rivers of ice. They start high up in the mountains, where it is cold. They flow down the mountain sides very slowly.

A glacier is made as snow builds up on the mountain side. When new snow falls it presses down on the layers under it. The old snow hardens into something between snow and ice. This is called **névé** (*nay-vay*).

The great weight of hard snow forms a hollow in the mountain side. The hollow is called **cirque** (*sirk*).

The path of a glacier

The névé pulls away from the upper edge of the cirque. A deep crack, or **crevasse**, is made there. At the lower edge, the névé begins to flow down the mountain. It hardens into ice. It has turned into a glacier.

Some glaciers travel only a few centimetres a day. Others travel several metres. As a glacier moves down the mountain, smaller glaciers join it.

◀ This glacier at Chamonix in France is moving slowly down the mountain. The ice cuts the rock away to make a deep valley. On the sides of the glacier you can see the rocks which have been torn away.

◀ The Yosemite Valley in California was shaped by glaciers. The ice made a deep, U-shaped valley. Half Dome Mountain, in the distance, was one of the only mountain peaks above the level of the ice.

▼ There are many fiords in Norway. You can see that the glacier cut a deep valley which ran right into the sea. Fiords are good and safe harbours for ships.

The sides of the glacier cut deeply into the mountain. They make a U-shaped valley. The glacier carries away pieces of rock. These rocks are left in lines along the sides of the valley. They are called **moraines**.

Lower down, where it is warmer, the ice begins to melt and flow as water. The end of the glacier is called its snout. There we find a great pile of rocks which the glacier has carried with it. This pile is called a **terminal** moraine.

The disappearing ice

Thousands of years ago the Earth's weather, or **climate**, was much colder than it is now. Huge ice caps covered large areas in the north and south of the world. From the South Pole the ice covered New Zealand and parts of South America. From the North Pole the ice covered a lot of Europe and North America.

The climate changed about 10 000 years ago. It grew warmer. The ice melted. The ice caps in the Arctic and Antarctic are all that is left today.

The ice left its mark on the land. U-shaped valleys can still be seen in the great mountain ranges.

Glaciers cut right into the sea bed in some places. When the glaciers melted, they left long, narrow fingers of deep water. These are called **fiords** (*fee-yawds*). It is a Norwegian word and many fiords can be seen in Norway. There are also fiords in Canada, Scotland, Chile and New Zealand.

Mountain climates

tree line

coniferous forest

rain forest

crops

As you go up Kilimanjaro in Tanzania the climate changes. It is hot at the foot of the mountain. Further up, in the coniferous forests, it is cooler. Above the tree line, it is too cold for trees to grow. The peak is always covered in snow.

The peaks of high mountains are covered with snow, even in the hottest parts of the world. If you climbed a mountain you would find it getting colder as you climbed higher. On the way, you would pass through different climates as the air got cooler and thinner. You would see different plants and animals at each level. The climate would change quite quickly as you climbed.

The climb begins

The widest range of mountain climates can be seen on a mountain near the **Equator**. Mount Kilimanjaro is in Tanzania in East Africa. It is only 350 km from the Equator. Its summit is 5895 m above sea level. It stands up from a wide, hot, dry plain. This is home for wildlife like zebras, giraffes and lions. Farmers keep cattle but they find it hard to grow crops there because there is little rain on the plain.

More rain falls on the lower slopes of the mountain. It is still very warm. Farmers grow coffee and bananas. Above this level, there is the warm, wet **rain forest**. At about 2400 m above sea level the climate becomes colder and drier. This is the level of the **coniferous forest**. Conifers are the only trees that can survive at that height. Higher up, above the **tree line**, no trees grow. It is cold, dry and windy on the bare mountain side. Only plants like grass will grow.

▲ The lower slopes of this mountain in the Alps are used for grazing and growing crops. Higher up, there is forest. Then the trees get smaller and there are fewer of them. There are no trees near the mountain peak. Only grass and special plants can survive.

Above the tree line

Above the tree line the air is thin. There is less oxygen. All living things need oxygen to stay alive. Plants that grow at this level have to be very tough to survive. They must be able to live without much water, as there is little rain. Any moisture in the air often falls as snow. Plants must adapt to survive there.

Alpine plants have adapted so they can grow high up on the mountain. Most of these plants grow close to the ground. They put down long roots in cracks between the rocks. Alpine plants often grow close together in clumps. This helps to protect them from the cold and wind.

Giant cacti also grow at this high level on Mount Kilimanjaro. They can store water in their barrel-like stems. These cacti are not found on many other mountains.

Higher up on the mountain, only mosses and **lichens** cling to the rocks. Above about 4600 m, the mountain is always covered with snow and ice. This level is called the snow line. Nothing can grow above this line.

Changing climates

Mountains that are further from the Equator than Mount Kilimanjaro have fewer levels because their climates are colder. The Sierra Nevada in the USA have no rain forest. They are too far north. Far from the Equator, the snow line is much lower because the climate at the foot of the mountains is much colder. In the mountains of Iceland the snow line is only 1000 m above sea level.

13

Mountain animals

True mountain animals live above the tree line. Many other kinds of animals live on the lower slopes. These are not really mountain animals as they can live in other places as well.

Living on the high slopes

The bodies of mountain animals have adapted to living on the high slopes. Insects find it very hard to fly in strong winds, so most mountain insects do not have wings. Those insects that do fly, stay close to the ground.

Mountain **mammals** have to be good climbers. Some of the best climbers are the wild goats and sheep. The Rocky Mountain goat is related to the chamois of the Alps and Pyrenees. The mouflon (*moo-flon*) is a sheep found in the mountains of Europe. The bighorn is a type of sheep found in the mountains of North America.

Mountain mammals have to get all the oxygen they need from the thin air. Some animals, like the vicuna, have large hearts and lungs. The vicuna lives in the Andes Mountains of South America. The vicuna's blood can carry extra oxygen around its body. This means that the vicuna can run at nearly 50 km an hour when it is as high as 4500 m. At that height, people and horses can hardly breathe.

◄ The ibex is a type of goat. It is very nimble, and can leap easily from rock to rock. The ibex lives high in the mountains of Europe.

The search for food

Many mountain animals are plant-eaters. Some birds eat seeds and some insects eat leaves. Many of the mammals eat grass and shrubs. These include smaller animals like the pika of the Himalayas and the chinchilla of the Andes. Sheep and goats also eat plants.

Larger animals, like the puma or mountain lion, hunt and kill the plant-eaters for food. They are called **predators**. The rare snow leopard lives in the mountains of Asia. It makes its home at heights of about 4500 m. It is a good climber and likes rocky places where it can creep up on its **prey**.

There are hunting birds, like the eagle owl of Europe and North Africa. This eats other birds and small mammals, like mice. The Andean condor floats over the mountains and looks out for dead animals, or **carrion**, to eat. It flies up to 7000 m high, yet it can see the ground below very clearly.

▼ The condor glides high above the Andes Mountains looking for food. Its wings can be more than three metres from tip to tip.

Survival in the winter

It is hard for mountain animals to stay alive in the winter. It is very cold. There is little food and it is hard to find under the snow and ice. Birds can fly away to warmer places. Most mammals move to the lower slopes of the mountain in the winter. The chamois moves down to shelter in the forest during the coldest winter months. A few animals, like the Rocky Mountain goat and the ibex, do move higher up the mountain. They look for places where the wind has blown the snow from the ground and uncovered their food.

Voles and other small mammals burrow under the snow to find grass to eat. It is warmer under the snow than in the open air. This also helps the animals to survive the cold.

The yak

The yak is a type of wild ox. It lives high in the mountains in Tibet and Mongolia. It is very well adapted to mountain life. The yak can survive as high as 6000 m above sea level. No other mammal can live at this height.

The yak's coat is always thick. In winter its coat grows so long that it almost touches the ground. The yak is a heavy animal, but it can climb among the steep rocks to look for its food. The yak eats mosses and lichens when it cannot find grass. It climbs to higher slopes in winter. There the wind has blown the snow away and the yak can find food. It will graze in a high wind in the snow. It can live in the cold, even when the **temperature** drops as low as −30°C.

▼ This herd of yaks is grazing on the snowy grass in Mongolia. The yak will eat mosses and lichens if it cannot find any grass. Its thick coat keeps it warm in the biting winds and the freezing cold.

► The Rocky Mountain goat lives above the tree line. The goat has very thick hair to keep it warm.

Living in the snow

Some animals use **camouflage** to survive. They change colour in the winter to match their surroundings.

The stoat is found in northern Europe. It is a hunter. In the winter the stoat changes colour from brown to white. Then it can creep up on its prey in the snow without being seen.

The snowshoe hare also turns white in the winter. It changes colour to stop hunters, like the stoat, from seeing it against the snow. The snowshoe hare also has wide, furry feet. These do not sink easily into the snow. Snowshoe hares are found in Europe and America.

The ptarmigan (*tar-mi-gan*) is a bird that lives in northern Europe. It also has snowshoes and turns white in the winter.

The ptarmigan grows thick skin and feathers on its feet. These help it to move across the deep snow.

Underground shelters

Some animals shelter from the cold by going under the ground. Bears make dens in caves. They sleep there most of the winter. On warmer days, they come out to look for food.

A few animals, like marmots, **hibernate** underground. The marmots dig a burrow and make a nest at the end of it. They line the nest with dry grass.

A few marmots curl up together in the nest all winter. Their body temperature drops. Their hearts slow down. They wake a few times during the winter, but they do not leave the burrow until the spring.

Mountains like walls

Mountains can act like walls or **barriers**. They keep types of plants and animals from spreading to another area with the same climate.

The mountain sides and tops are usually far away from people. The climate allows plants and animals that cannot live anywhere else to live on the mountains. There is a plant called the giant groundsel which is found only on the slopes of Mount Kenya.

Divided by the mountains

In Asia, mountains divide the south of the continent from the north. The chains of mountains run from the Caucasus in the west to the Himalayas in the east. Warm wet winds, called **monsoons**, blow from the south. Most rain falls on the warm south side of the mountains. The wind cools as it rises over them. The lands on the north side, like Siberia and the Gobi Desert, are dry and cold. They are in the **rain shadow** of the mountains.

Mountains can keep animals within an area or **range**. Some animals cannot get over or round a chain of mountains.

The animals of southern Asia, like monkeys and elephants, cannot cross the mountain barrier. They could not live in the colder climate on the other side. The animals to the north of the mountains, like the yak, are quite different. They could not live in the warmer climate to the south.

▲ This plant is a giant groundsel. It grows high up on the slopes of Mount Kenya in East Africa.

▶ These mountains are part of Australia's Great Dividing Range. The Great Dividing Range stretches down the eastern side of Australia for about 3600 km. The mountains are close to the coast. They stop the rain-carrying winds from the coast from moving inland. Much of central Australia is dry because of this.

▲ This Dall sheep is one of many types of bighorn sheep. It lives high in the Rocky Mountains in Canada.

North and South America

Huge mountain chains run from north to south near the west coast of North and South America. The animals in these mountains have a wide range. The climate above the tree line is the same for hundreds of kilometres.

The pika is related to the rabbit. It lives above the tree line in the North American mountains. The pika can live as far north as Alaska and as far south as New Mexico.

Other animals used to share this wide range. The bighorn sheep used to live in the mountains from Canada in the north to Mexico in the south. It too lived above the tree line. People have driven the bighorn away from many areas. Now it lives only in small areas of the mountains, far away from people.

Mountains of fire

Volcanoes are holes, or **vents**, in the Earth's crust. They lead down to the liquid magma deep inside the Earth. Sometimes, hot gases and magma push their way up through the vent. When this happens the volcano **erupts**.

The hot magma that is pushed out is called **lava**. Rocks and ash are also thrown up in the eruption. The rocks and ash make a mountain around the vent. Volcanoes can also be made under the sea. Some grow high enough to reach above the water. They become islands. Tristan da Cunha in the Atlantic Ocean is an island volcano.

Types of volcano

An **active** volcano is one that sometimes erupts. There are about 850 active volcanoes in the world today. About 80 are on the sea bed. There are 30 to 40 volcanic eruptions each year. Volcanoes which have not erupted for many years are sleeping, or **dormant**, volcanoes. Volcanoes that will never erupt again are **extinct**.

Some volcanoes push out very stiff lava. This quickly becomes solid around the vent. The layers of dried lava and ash make a pointed **cone** shape with the vent at the top.

Not all volcanoes are cone-shaped. If the lava is not very stiff, it will flow away easily. It hardens slowly. The lava makes a low mountain called a **shield**. The best known shield volcano is Mauna Loa in Hawaii. Mauna Loa often erupts but it is never very violent.

◄ This volcano in Hawaii is erupting. Burning ash and smoke are flying into the air. Lava is pouring down the side of the mountain.

Famous eruptions

Sometimes the lava hardens in the vent. It makes a plug. The magma and hot gas build up in the volcano but the plug stops it erupting. In the end, the mountain explodes.

A famous eruption happened in Indonesia, in 1883. A volcano called Krakatoa blew itself apart. People could hear the explosion 4000 km away. It sent a huge wave across the sea. The wave flooded nearby islands and killed 36 000 people.

A few years later, in 1902, Mount Pelée in Martinique erupted. The side of the mountain exploded. The lava plug was left behind. A cloud of ash, steam and burning gas rolled down the mountain. It destroyed the nearby town of St Pierre. Everyone was killed except a murderer in his prison cell.

Often scientists can tell when a volcano is going to erupt. People have time to escape. Sometimes people take no notice of the warnings. They do not want to leave their homes. This is what happened when Mount Pelée erupted.

▲ This church is on the top of a hill made of lava. The hill is the plug of a volcano at Le Puy in France. The rest of the volcano has been eroded.

A cone volcano is made up of layers of lava and ash.

A Pelean volcano is named after Mount Pelée. This volcano erupts violently.

A Strombolian volcano erupts very often, like the volcano in Italy called Stromboli. The eruptions are rarely violent.

A shield volcano erupts gently almost all the time. It pours out a stream of thin lava.

The Ring of Fire

▼ There was a huge explosion when Mount St Helens erupted. There is now a large hollow where part of the mountain top was blown off. Black lava and ash covered the forests and killed the trees.

Some parts of the Earth's crust are weaker than others. The weakest parts are often where the edges of the plates meet. Most of the world's volcanoes are at these weak points.

All around the Pacific Ocean, the edges of the plates are being pushed down into the magma. Sometimes the magma is pushed upwards and a volcano is made. Look at the map on page 24. You will see how the volcanoes around the Pacific form a ring. Some of the most active of the world's volcanoes are in this ring. It is called the Ring of Fire. The famous Japanese volcano, Fujiyama, is in this ring.

Mount St Helens

In the last few years there have been two very large eruptions on the eastern side of the Ring of Fire. Mount St Helens in Washington State, USA, exploded on 17 May 1980.

Mount St Helens had been sending out gas, steam and ash for three months before it erupted. Not all of the gas could escape. Some of it built up inside the mountain. The north side began to bulge. An **earthquake** shook and weakened the mountain enough for the gas to push its way out. It blew off one side of the mountain.

The noise was so loud that people heard it 500 km away. Hot gases and steam destroyed trees in forests up to 30 km away. A huge cloud of ash blocked out the sun. When the ash and rocks fell, farmland was ruined. Many people and animals were choked to death.

▶ Some volcanoes are quite new. In 1943, a volcano began in a field near the village of Paricutin in Mexico. There were many violent eruptions. In nine years the volcano grew to a height of 410 m. The lava buried the nearby village of Las Colchas, except for the top of the church, which you can see in the picture. Plants soon started to grow again.

Disaster in the Andes

The other large eruption was in the Andes. Nevado del Ruiz is a volcano in Colombia. It erupted on 14 November 1985. There had been no serious eruptions for 390 years. People called the mountain 'the sleeping giant'. Towns had grown up nearby and people farmed the land around. Scientists warned the people that it might erupt but most people did not want to leave their farms and homes.

The 1985 eruption was worse than anyone had expected. Snow and ice from the top of the volcano melted. The water mixed with the soil on the mountain side and formed thick mud. The mud slid down the mountain into the valley below. It buried almost the whole town of Armero. About 20 000 people were killed.

The job of rescuing the people was difficult. The mud made it impossible to reach Armero by road. There were few places for helicopters to land. People were cold and wet. They had no food or clean water. They had lost their homes, their land, their families and friends.

Mountains and volcanoes

The highest mountains in the world are the Himalayas and the Karakorams in Asia. Many of the mountain peaks there are over 7500 m above sea level. The highest mountain in the world is Mount Everest. It is 8848 m above sea level. The first climbers reached the top of Everest in 1953. They were Sir Edmund Hillary from New Zealand and his Sherpa guide, Tensing Norgay. The first woman to climb Everest in 1975 was Junko Tabei, from Japan.

The weather on mountains can be very bad. The strongest wind in the world has been measured on Mount Washington in the USA. A wind speed of 371 kph was

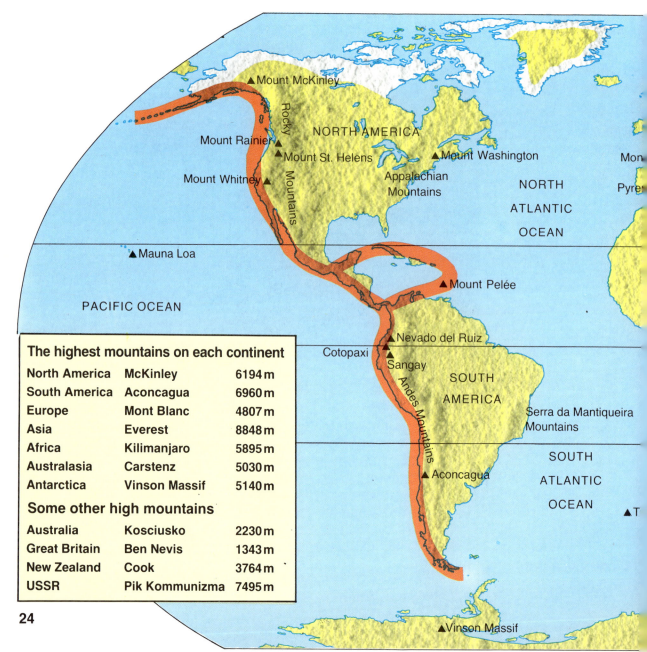

The highest mountains on each continent

North America	McKinley	6194 m
South America	Aconcagua	6960 m
Europe	Mont Blanc	4807 m
Asia	Everest	8848 m
Africa	Kilimanjaro	5895 m
Australasia	Carstenz	5030 m
Antarctica	Vinson Massif	5140 m

Some other high mountains

Australia	Kosciusko	2230 m
Great Britain	Ben Nevis	1343 m
New Zealand	Cook	3764 m
USSR	Pik Kommunizma	7495 m

recorded in 1934. The biggest fall of snow in the world was also on a mountain in the USA. More than 30 m of snow fell on Mount Rainier, in Washington State, in one year.

Mount Waialeale is on the island of Kauai in the Pacific Ocean. There are up to 350 rainy days a year on the mountain. It is said to be the wettest place in the world.

Volcanoes

The island of Hawaii is made up of five volcanoes. One of these is Mauna Loa. It is the widest active volcano in the world.

The highest active volcano is in the Andes. Cotopaxi is 5897 m above sea level. The most active volcano is Sangay, also in the Andes. Sangay was found by explorers over 400 years ago. The volcano has erupted gently nearly every day since then.

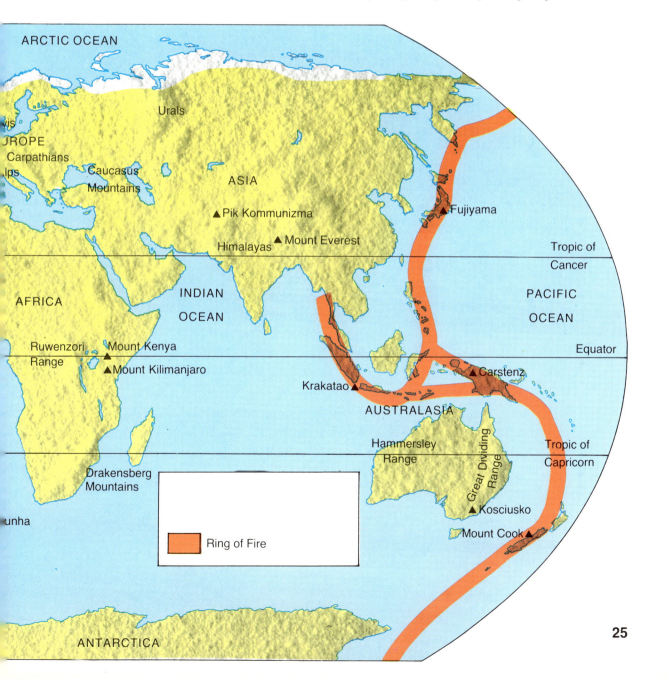

25

The Incas

The Incas were people who lived high in the Andes. They came from the area around Cuzco which today is in Peru.

From about 1438 the Incas set out to rule the land and people around them. Soon they controlled most of the Andes Mountains. The Inca **empire** stretched along most of the west coast of South America. The Incas were rich and powerful, but their empire lasted only about 100 years.

▲ These are the ruins of the Inca city of Machu Picchu. The city was built on terraces cut into the rock. You can see the large blocks of stone which the Incas used to build their houses.

▲ The Inca empire stretched for about 3200 km from north to south. It went along the west coast of South America and inland through the Andes Mountains. Roads linked each part of the empire with the capital, Cuzco.

The rulers

The first Inca ruler was called Manco Capac. The Incas believed he was made by the sun god on an island in Lake Titicaca.

An Inca ruler had great power. He made rules about how people should live. His **officials** made sure the ruler's orders were carried out. They also shared out the land among the people so everyone had enough land to grow food.

Buildings and roads

The Incas built cities of stone in the mountains. They had few tools but they were able to cut stone blocks which fitted together very well. The ruins of their city, Machu Picchu, show what good builders they were. It is said that they covered some of their buildings with gold.

The ruler's officials needed to travel around the empire to make sure the people were obeying the rules, so the Incas built two paved highways. One highway went along the coast, one went through the mountains. Smaller roads ran between them. The roads were built in zig-zags up the steep slopes. Sometimes the builders cut steps into the mountain side. People travelled on foot. They used llamas to carry goods. The Incas did not use carts because they did not know about the wheel.

The village people

Most Inca people were farmers. Many farmed the steep mountain slopes. They grew crops on huge steps, called **terraces**, cut out of the mountain side. They grew food for the sun god, the ruler and for themselves. After a bad harvest, the officials shared out food from the ruler's stores. No one went hungry.

People ate mostly vegetables. Their main crops were maize and potatoes. They dried some of their crops, so they had enough food for the winter. In the high mountains, people used to freeze potatoes in snow, so they would keep for a long time.

Very few people ate meat. Llamas and alpacas were kept for their wool and to carry goods. The people near the coast grew cotton. The Inca women were very good weavers. They **dyed** the wool and the cotton in bright colours. Then they used them to weave patterns in their cloth.

The end of the empire

A Spanish general named Francisco Pizarro reached the Inca empire with a small army in 1532. He had heard the Incas were rich and that they had gold. The general wanted to take the gold back to Spain. The Incas had been fighting amongst themselves and the empire had become weak. The Spanish army defeated the Incas very easily. The Spaniards killed the Incas' ruler and took over his empire. They made the people give up their way of life and become Christians. The Spaniards also took a huge amount of gold back to Spain.

▼ These Quechua Indians are sowing potatoes and ploughing the land in the Andes Mountains. Their way of life has changed very little for hundreds of years.

Hidden in the mountains

People who live in mountain areas are often cut off from the outside world. Travel is hard and there are few visitors. New ideas take a long time to reach them, so people keep to their old, or **traditional**, way of life.

The Quechua (*kech-wa*) people of the Andes are **descendants** of the Incas. Their way of life has stayed much the same for hundreds of years. They still keep llamas and grow potatoes. They live in the same kind of houses as the Incas. They weave the wool of llamas and alpacas just like the Incas.

There have been some changes to the old way of life. The Spanish taught the people about Christianity. Most of the Quechua people are Christians. People now keep sheep as well as llamas. Many places can be reached by road or by railway. The children go to school in the villages. The people know more about the outside world than the Incas.

Taking to the mountains

Many mountain peoples first made their homes in the mountains in order to be safe. The people of Lesotho in southern Africa did this. Over 100 years ago, there was a war in the area where they used to live. There was also little food, or a **famine**. Their first leader, Moshweshwe, led his people to a safe new home in the Drakensberg Mountains.

Some people have gone to the mountains to get away from everyday life. **Monasteries** may be built in far away places. There, the monks can work and pray in peace. There are some monasteries in the Meteora area in Greece.

◀ These people live in the remote mountains of Papua New Guinea. The mountains act as a barrier between them and the outside world.

◀ The kingdom of Lesotho lies in the middle of South Africa. There are many villages like this on the mountain slopes. In the distance, you can see where the people have cut terraces for growing crops.

▼ The mountains helped to keep people away from this Greek monastery. The monks used the wooden balcony on the left of the picture to pull people up in baskets. Now you can see there are steps cut into the rock.

The monasteries are over 600 years old. At one time, visitors could reach them only by climbing a rope ladder, or by the monks pulling people up in baskets. Now steps have been cut into the mountain.

People can hide in mountains. They have been used by bands of thieves and by **guerrilla** armies all over the world.

Mountain giants

Some strange stories, or **legends**, have been told by mountain people. The stories are about giant animals that may live in the mountains. One of these giants is said to be like a huge ape with red hair. Americans call it Bigfoot. In the Himalayas, the people talk of the giant called the yeti, or 'bearman'. Some people say they have seen his footprints in the snow. No one is certain if these giant animals are real or not. They could be hidden in the mountains.

Crossing the mountains

People have always tried to cross mountains. They hoped to find new lands to live in, or new goods to trade. Sometimes people just wanted to see what was on the other side.

People used animals to help them carry their goods. In the highest mountains the animals had to cope with the cold and thin air. Yaks and llamas have been used as pack animals for hundreds of years.

Some animals are not suited to mountain travel. In 218 BC Hannibal led an army to attack Italy. He wanted to make a surprise attack on the Romans. He marched across the Alps in the winter with a large army of men and horses, and 37 elephants. Only one elephant lived. Many men and horses died. However, the plan worked. The Romans did not expect an attack to come from the north.

▲ The Khyber Pass cuts through the mountains between Afghanistan and Pakistan. The road winds through the high valley.

Mountain passes

When people wanted to cross a mountain range, they looked for a **pass**. This is a valley between the peaks of a mountain range. People who had control of a pass could decide who could use it. They could also make travellers pay to cross.

The Khyber is a famous pass between Pakistan and Afghanistan. It is 50 km long, but at one point it is only 3 km wide.

Many armies have marched through it. The Persians used it in the 6th century BC. The Greeks marched through it in the 3rd century BC. The British built forts along it over 100 years ago. They wanted to protect their army from attack.

Crossing North America

The first European settlers in North America stayed on the east side of the Appalachian Mountains. Fur trappers were the first Europeans to cross this range over 200 years ago. They travelled on horseback and hunted for food. They also traded with the American Indians. The Indians had lived there long before the trappers arrived.

After 1840, more people crossed the mountains. They went west in search of new land and gold. They followed the routes the trappers had taken. Some people travelled in wagons pulled by oxen. Others went on foot or on horseback. These settlers took everything with them, even their farm animals. Some made their homes on the plains. Others went on to settle on the west coast of North America.

The journey from the plains to the west coast was not easy. The settlers had to cross the mountains which stretch down the west side of North America. These include the Rocky Mountains and the Sierra Nevada. The tracks through these mountains were rough and dangerous. Sometimes the wagons had to go along narrow ledges. There was often a steep drop on one side. The settlers had to watch out for rocks falling on to them from the mountain sides. Food was hard to find. People became ill. Winter was the worst time.

The first railway was built across the mountains in 1869. The railway began at Omaha, in Nebraska. It ended at Sacramento in California. Travel became easier. Today, people can fly over the mountains in planes.

▼ The early settlers in North America found it hard to cross the mountains and travel west. Mountain tracks were steep and narrow. Sometimes a wagon would fall over the edge.

Life in the mountains

People have lived high in the mountains for thousands of years. Like the mountain animals, people's bodies have adapted to the climate and the thin air. These people have large hearts and lungs. These things help them to take in enough oxygen from the thin air and to use it well. People who live in the Andes can work with ease at 4000 m above sea level. People who visit these high mountains run out of breath after just a short walk. The lack of oxygen in the air can make them feel ill.

The Sherpa people of Nepal are also used to living at a great height. They are skilled climbers. For many years they have been famous as porters and guides for people climbing in the Himalayas.

Village life

Most mountain people live in small groups. There is not enough work or food for a lot of people. Many people are farmers. They grow crops on the lower slopes. Some farmers also keep animals on the higher slopes. The farmers eat most of the crops that they grow and the food from their animals. A few people work in the village as builders or carpenters.

Some people who live in the mountains have other jobs. They may work in the forests. There are also jobs looking after tourists or in ski **resorts**.

Children who live high in the mountain may have to walk a very long way to school. If they go on to college, they usually have to live away from home.

▼ These Sherpas have been gathering firewood. They can carry heavy loads in the thin mountain air. People from lower down the mountains find this very difficult. Sherpas often work carrying loads for mountaineers in the Himalayas.

► This village is high in the Swiss Alps. The houses are all made of wood. You can see stacks of timber by the road.

▼ This village is 3400 m above sea level in Nepal. The Sherpas are buying cloth at the market. You can see that they wear many layers of clothes. They nearly all wear hats. The animals are kept close to the houses. The doors are wide enough to get the animals inside the houses during the winter. The small windows help to keep the houses warm in the winter.

Mountain homes

On the lower slopes of the mountains there are trees. People can build their homes with wood. There are few trees higher up the mountain. People there often use stone to build their homes.

The shape of the house is important. Houses in the Alps have long sloping roofs which hang down over the walls. The roof stops the snow falling on the doors and windows. People store firewood against the walls, under the roof. This keeps it dry.

In the Himalayas, the Sherpa people live as high as 4000 m above sea level. The ground floor of their houses is used to shelter their cattle. The people live up above the animals. The heat from the animals' bodies helps keep the houses warm.

Many mountain homes have thick walls and tiny windows. Large windows would let out too much heat in the cold winter. The thick walls keep the heat in during the winter. They also help to keep the houses cool in the summer.

People and animals

▼ The Quechua Indians are mountain people. They live near Cuzco in Peru. They need these llamas for many things. The woman on the left is spinning llama wool by hand. She is making yarn to weave into cloth.

Animals have always been very important to mountain people. Animals can be kept where few crops will grow. The animals provide food and their wool can be made into cloth. They can also be used to carry people and goods. Animals do not need to travel on roads. In some places, the animals' survival means the life or death of the people. So their animals are very valuable to them.

Animals for mountain farmers

Sheep and goats are kept by many mountain farmers. These animals are well suited to mountain life. They give people wool, meat, milk and skins for rugs and coats.

The people of the Himalayas keep yaks. Yaks are good pack animals. They can find their way across rough mountain slopes and they can carry loads of up to 100 kg.

Traders use yaks to carry their goods over long distances. **Nomads** are people who do not settle in one place. They move with their herds of animals, looking for food. The herdsmen use yaks to carry their tents and all their belongings. Yak meat can be eaten. The hide is made into clothes or tents. Yak dung is dried and used for fuel.

Llamas are used to carry loads in the Andes Mountains. Llamas are not as strong as yaks. The most that a llama can carry is about 50 kg. If it thinks the load is too heavy, it will just sit down and refuse to move. Llamas move in a very bumpy way. Their loads have to be tied on firmly. Llama fat is sometimes melted down and used to make candles. Llama wool is rough. It is made into sacking or rope. People get finer wool for cloth from the alpaca. This animal is related to the llama but the alpaca is smaller.

▲ These cows have spent the summer in the high mountain pastures of the Swiss Alps. The herdsman is taking them down to the valley below for the winter.

The search for fresh grass

Mountain people adapt their lives to suit their herds. Some Sherpa herdsmen leave their homes for the whole summer. They move with their yak herds. The yaks graze on the fresh grass, or **pasture**, high in the mountains.

In the Alps and in Norway, the best pastures in the summer are high up on the mountain slopes. The herdsmen move to simple huts or houses near these high pastures. The crops are grown near their homes in the valleys. Some people in the family stay there to look after the crops. In the winter, the herdsmen come home. They bring their animals down into the valleys. There the animals are kept indoors, out of the cold weather. This way of farming is called **transhumance**.

Farming the mountains

It is not easy to grow many crops in the mountains. The soil is poor. The weather is cold and the summers are often short. Only a few crops will grow in this **environment**. In the Andes, the Quechuas grow beans, potatoes and barley. These crops are also grown in the Himalayas as well as buckwheat and millet. People who use all the crops they grow are called **subsistence** farmers.

▲ This volcano is on Lanzarote, a part of the Canary Islands near northern Africa. The farmers have made fields on the lower slopes because the soil around a volcano is very fertile.

◄ These people are picking tea in Japan. The tea plants grow well on the warm and sheltered lower slopes of the mountains.

The lower slopes

It is much easier to grow crops on the lower slopes of mountains. The climate is warmer and the land is more sheltered. There is often plenty of rain. The soil is good. In warm countries, the lower slopes are good places to grow tea and coffee. The lower slopes of the Himalayas are famous for their crops of tea. Brazil grows most of the world's coffee. Most of the coffee grows on the slopes of the Serra da Mantiqueira Mountains, near the Atlantic Ocean. In the cooler areas of Europe and North America, crops, like grapes and oranges, are often planted on sunny mountain slopes. People grow these crops to sell, rather than to feed their families. They are called **cash crops**.

Working the land

It is more difficult to plant crops on mountain slopes, than on flat land. On very steep slopes, tractors and other machines cannot be used. The people have to do the work themselves using **hand tools**. They use their animals to pull ploughs.

In parts of Asia, farmers grow rice on the mountain sides. Rice fields are called paddies. They have to be flooded for part of the year. Farmers make terraces which can hold water, so that each paddy can be flooded. They make sure that water reaches the plants by using a system of ditches. Carrying water to crops in this way is called **irrigation**. The terraces also stop the soil being washed away, or **eroded**, when rain falls or the crops are watered.

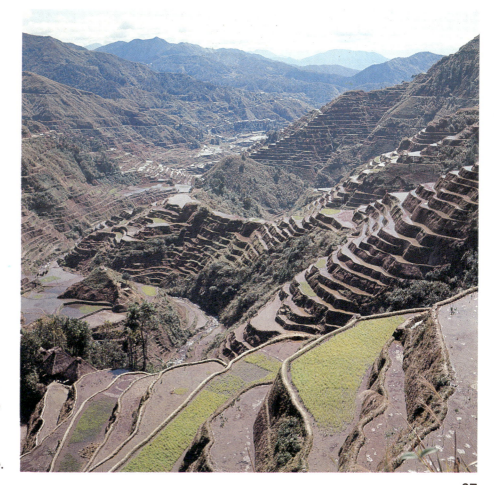

▶ You can see the green rice plants growing on some of these terraces in the Philippines. The ground has to be flooded for part of the year to grow rice.

Using the mountains

The cash crops grown in the mountains are sent around the world to feed people. Mountains give other things that people use. Trees provide wood for building and to make paper. Some mountains are rich in **minerals** which we use in industry. The power from mountain rivers can be used to make **electricity**.

Forests

There are huge areas of coniferous forest in the world. Much of it is in the mountains of Alaska, Canada, the USSR and Scandinavia. The wood from coniferous trees is called softwood. It is used for building and to make furniture. Softwood can also be made into paper.

The trees that grow on the lower slopes of **tropical** mountains near the Equator are hardwoods. Some hardwoods are also used for building and to make furniture.

People whose job is to cut down trees are called lumberjacks. Felling trees used to be very hard work, as only hand tools were used. Today, people use machines like chain saws. These machines make the job easier, but it is still hard and dangerous work.

Forests are also cut down so that crops can be grown on the land. Trees help to keep the soil from being eroded. People today take care to replace some of the trees to stop erosion.

Riches in the mountains

Many metals are found in the mountains. Gold was found in the Sierra Nevada in North America about 150 years ago. People came from all over the world to mine the gold. The towns they built are

◄ Mount Tom Price is in Western Australia. It is made of iron ore. It is slowly disappearing as the iron ore is mined. You can see the trucks and the railway which take the iron away.

still there, but the people have gone. They are called 'ghost towns'.

Silver is mined from the mountains in Mexico and in Peru. Iron and copper are both used a great deal in industry. Much of the world's iron and copper is mined in the mountains. A large amount of iron ore comes from the Hammersley Range in Australia. Iron can be made into steel. Knives, tools and machines are made from steel.

Nearly half of the world's copper is in the Andes Mountains in Chile. There are also copper mines in Australia and in the Urals in the USSR. Most copper in the USA comes from mines in New Mexico and Arizona.

Water from the mountains

The power of water rushing down from the mountains can be used by people. A strong wall, or **dam**, is built across a river. The water makes a lake, or **reservoir**, behind the dam. The stored water can be used for drinking, for watering crops and for making electricity.

Electricity made using the power of falling water is called **hydro-electricity**. A gate in the dam is opened. Water from the lake rushes through. It hits a wheel with blades on it, called a **turbine**. The turbine turns the machines which make electricity.

The Snowy Mountains Project in Australia is an example of how rivers can be used to make electricity and to water the land. Several rivers begin in the Snowy Mountains. Sixteen large dams were built across the rivers. The water can now irrigate land many kilometres away. The dams are also used to make hydro-electric power. Australia gets nearly one-fifth of its electricity from hydro-electric power.

▼ The Glen Canyon Dam is on the Colorado River, in Arizona. The lake behind the dam is storing water that has flowed from the Rocky Mountains.

Travel in the mountains

People need to be able to carry goods through mountain ranges. Long ago, people and their animals used paths through mountain passes. The journey was slow. The animals could not carry much. Now it is much easier to travel in the mountains using roads and railways.

Railways were built in many mountain areas long before the roads. Many of the railways were built 100 years ago. The Canadian Pacific Railway was finished in 1885. After that, many people travelled by rail and settled in western Canada. In the USA, railways ran through the Rocky Mountains and Sierra Nevada. This meant that people could reach the west coast quickly and safely.

Now there are good roads through some mountain ranges. Railways are still needed. One train can carry more goods than many trucks. It is easier to keep railways working in the snow.

Through the Alps

Over 100 years ago the great railway builders had to find a way to build a railway line across the Alps. The Alps are very steep. Trains cannot go up very steep slopes.

To make the climb easier for the trains the railway lines were built in **spirals**. The lines went through a series of tunnels as they wound up the mountain side. Then the railway lines went through long tunnels under the mountain peaks. **Viaducts** were also built to take the lines across the deep valleys.

The St Gotthard line runs from Lucerne in Switzerland to Milan in Italy. It crosses 79 bridges and viaducts and it goes through

▲ Roads have to be built in zig-zags up the steep sides of mountains. The sharp bends are sometimes called 'hairpin' bends. These roads are often blocked by ice and snow in the winter.

▶ Mountain railways like this one are hard to build. Before trains can run, a tunnel has to be dug through the mountain. Then a viaduct has to be built to cross the valley.

► This steam train is still working on the Central Line in Peru. The engine was built in England nearly 40 years ago.

81 tunnels. The St Gotthard tunnel is one of the longest. It is 15 km long. The tunnel took 2500 people ten years to build. They worked in two teams, one from each side of the mountain. They often used simple hand tools, such as picks, although they had drills as well. When the two parts of the tunnel met in the middle of the mountain, they found there was only a few centimetres difference between the two parts. The tunnel was completed in 1880.

The Simplon is another famous tunnel through the Alps. It was finished in 1906. It runs under the Simplon Pass. The tunnel is nearly 20 km long. It is one of the longest railway tunnels in the world. At one point, it is 2100 m under the ground. Today, there are also road tunnels through the Alps.

Through the Andes

The Central Line in Peru runs from Lima, near the coast, up into the Andes. Its highest point is 4818 m above sea level. This makes it one of the highest railway lines in the world. The line was built in the 1880s. The town at the end of the line is Huancavelica. It used to be an important mining town when the line was first opened.

It took 23 years to build the Central Line. There are 66 tunnels and 59 bridges. The line has to zig-zag on ledges up the steep slopes. At the end of each straight part of the line the train stops. Then it is driven backwards up the next part of the zig-zag. The train goes so high that some passengers find it hard to breathe. There is oxygen on board if they need it.

Mountain sports

Many people began to visit the mountains when the new roads and railways were built. It was much easier to reach the mountain peaks. Many people enjoy summer walking holidays in the mountains. Today, many people also spend their winter holidays in the mountains. Most of them go skiing.

▼ A cable car is taking people to the top of Sugar Loaf Mountain in Rio de Janeiro, Brazil. It is a quick and easy way to get up a mountain. People also use cable cars when they are skiing in the mountains.

Winter sports

Skating, bobsleighing and skiing are all winter sports. Most people like fast, downhill skiing best.

In Europe, North America and Australia, mountain villages and towns have become ski resorts. New hotels, shops and cafes have been built for people on holiday. There are also schools to teach people to ski. Cable cars and ski lifts take people up the mountains. Cable cars are like buses which hang from cables above the mountain slopes. Ski lifts are like chairs which hang on cables just above the ground.

Many people have found work in the ski resorts of Europe. In the USA too, there are many winter sports resorts in the Rocky Mountains, the Sierra Nevada,

◄ Many people take skiing holidays in the winter. These children are learning to ski on the nursery slopes near the village.

▼ Some people enjoy climbing mountains like Mont Blanc between France and Italy. They have to learn to climb safely. They take special equipment.

and in the mountains of New England. The best ski resorts in Australia are found in the Australian Alps. These mountains are between Melbourne and Sydney. They are part of Australia's Great Dividing Range.

Climbing the mountains

The sport of mountain climbing began in the Alps about 200 years ago. The early mountaineers used long sticks with spikes on the end, called pikes, and boots with metal studs. They climbed some of the highest peaks, like the Matterhorn and Mont Blanc. The sport soon spread to other countries.

Today, climbers carry ropes, tents, ice picks and hooks. They wear special clothes. Climbers fix sharp points called crampons to their boots to help their feet grip the ice. People need all these things when they climb the world's toughest mountains. Climbing is a dangerous sport. Every year, climbers fall and are killed or injured.

The mystery of mountains

▼ The snow leopard of the Himalayas is very rare. People hunted the snow leopard for its fur. It nearly died out. Now there is a law to stop people hunting it.

High mountain ranges are some of the few parts of the world that have not been spoiled. They have always been hard to get to. Plants, animals and people have been able to live there in peace.

Looking after the mountains

Many mountain areas have already been spoiled. The slopes have been badly farmed. The soil has been washed away. Roads and mines have cut into the mountains. Plants have been killed. Animals have lost their homes.

Many countries are trying to look after their mountain areas. They are making them into national parks. These are places where wildlife can live without being harmed by people. There are few new buildings and roads in these parks. People may visit the parks, but they have to obey the rules. The needs of the wildlife in the park come first. Yellowstone Park in the Rocky Mountains is one of the best known national parks.

Mountain gods

People have always found mountains strange and special places. They are so high and far away from most villages and towns. Mountains are often covered with cloud and snow. People felt that such places must be the homes of gods and spirits.

The people of ancient Greece believed that their gods lived on Mount Olympus, in northern Greece. Some people in the Andes and the Himalayas still feel that there are spirits in the mountains that can help or hurt them. The Kikuyu people of Mount Kenya also feel that their mountain is a holy place.

The future

Today, travel in the mountains is easier than ever before. More and more people want to visit them. Life in the mountains is changing. Farms, forests, mines and dams have already changed the look of the land. We do not know how long mountains will remain strange or special places.

▲ These walkers are 'back packing' in the mountains of Alberta, Canada. These mountains and the wildlife are protected. They are part of the Jasper National Park.

▼ Fujiyama in Japan is a volcano with an almost perfect cone shape. There is snow on the mountain peak all year round. Some people believe the mountain is holy.

Glossary

active: describes a volcano which sometimes sends out hot liquid rock from the Earth beneath

adapt: to change in order to suit different surroundings

Alpine: (1) to do with the Alps. (2) describes plants or animals that are well suited to living high up in mountains

barrier: something that keeps people or animals apart

block mountain: a mountain made when a part of the Earth's outer shell is pushed up and stands above the surrounding land

camouflage: the ability of some animals to look like their surroundings

carrion: the flesh of a dead animal

cash crop: a crop which people grow to sell rather than to use themselves

chain: several lines of mountains running next to each other

cirque: a bowl-shaped hollow in a mountain side. It is cut out by the pressure of snow and ice

climate: the usual weather conditions found in an area

collide: to strike violently together

cone: a solid shape which has a circle at one end and a point at the other

coniferous forest: a type of forest made up of trees called conifers. They have needle-like leaves and produce woody cones which protect their seeds. They keep their leaves all year round

continent: a large piece of land, sometimes including many countries. The Earth is divided into seven continents

core: the centre of something

crevasse: a deep split in the ice on a mountain side

crust: the outer shell of the Earth

dam: a strong wall built to hold back a river

delta: a fan-shaped area of land made by the mud, sand and stones dropped at a river mouth. The river divides into many channels as it flows through the delta to the sea

descendant: someone who has come from an earlier member of a family or group of people

dissolve: to melt or break up

dormant: a state of not being in action, or sleeping. A dormant volcano has not erupted for many years but may do so one day

drainage system: a group of streams or rivers which carry away all the water from a large area and meet to flow together into the sea

dye: to give new colour to something

earthquake: a sudden shaking of the Earth's surface due to movements in the liquid rock beneath

electricity: a kind of energy or power, used to heat and light homes, run factories and do many other jobs

empire: several countries or groups of people all ruled by one person

environment: the surroundings of animals or plants. The environment affects the way an animal lives

Equator: the imaginary circle which goes around the middle of the Earth. The hottest parts of the world are nearest to the Equator

erode: to wear away the land by water, ice and wind

erosion: the wearing away of land by water, ice and wind

erupt: to send out liquid rock, smoke and ashes. Volcanoes erupt when pressure builds up underneath the Earth's surface

expand: to get bigger

extinct: (1) describes a type of animal or plant that has died out. (2) describes a volcano that will not erupt again

famine: a time of a great lack of food in a country because of a disaster like a bad harvest

fault: a crack in the outer shell of the Earth. Faults happen when a block of land is pushed up, sinks down or moves sideways

fiord: a long, narrow piece of sea between high cliffs or mountains

fold mountain: a mountain made when the outer shell of the Earth is pushed up and bent over. The tops of the bends become mountains

fossil: the remains of an animal or plant, usually found in rocks. A fossil may be the bones of an animal, or the shape left by the animal's body in the rock

glacier: a slow-moving river of ice

guerrilla: describes a group of fighters, usually fighting against a country's regular army

hand tool: an instrument, held in the hand, which helps someone do something

hibernate: to sleep deeply or stay still through the winter. Animals hibernate so that they can survive the cold weather and when food is scarce

hydro-electricity: electricity made using the power of falling water

irrigation: a way of bringing water by pipe or river, to land that has little rain. Crops can grow on irrigated land

lava: hot, liquid rock that flows from deep inside the Earth. The lava cools and hardens when it comes to the surface

legend: a popular old story, supposed to be true

lichen: a slow-growing hardy plant that can live on very little food and water. Lichens grow mostly on trees and rocks

magma: melted rock beneath the Earth's crust

mammal: an animal with a warm body which is usually covered in fur. Mammals give birth to live young which feed on the mother's milk

mantle: a layer of the Earth that lies between the outer shell and the central part

mineral: any material dug from the Earth by mining. Gold, coal and diamonds are minerals

monastery: a place where monks live, work and pray

monsoon: a strong wind that changes direction according to the season. Monsoons bring heavy rain to South East Asia in the summer

moraine: a line or pile of broken rock carried along and left behind by a glacier

névé: snow that has been pressed into small hard grains while lying on the ground

nomads: people who move about from place to place and do not make their homes in one particular place

official: a person in charge of something

oxygen: a gas found in the air and in the water, which all animals need for breathing

pass: a route between high mountains

pasture: a piece of land covered in grass

peak: the top of a pointed mountain

plate: a section of the Earth's outer shell. It floats like a raft on the liquid rock beneath

predator: an animal which lives by hunting and eating other animals

prey: an animal which is hunted and eaten by other animals for food

rain forest: a type of forest of large-leaved trees growing in a warm, wet climate

rain shadow: an area of little rain on the side of a mountain furthest from the sea

range: (1) a line of mountains. (2) the area over which a kind of animal or plant can be found. The marmot's range is above the snow line on mountain slopes

reservoir: a lake which builds up behind a dam. A reservoir is used for collecting and storing water

resort: a place to which people go for a holiday

scree: pieces of rock that have piled up at the bottom of mountain slopes

sea level: the height that the sea reaches halfway between low tide and high tide

shield: a low, rounded volcano made when lava flows away quickly before it hardens

spiral: a shape or line that curves around and around while moving away from a point

subsistence: a kind of farming. Subsistence farmers usually have small pieces of land and grow food mainly for themselves and their families

survive: to stay alive

temperature: the measure of how hot or cold something is

terminal: of or at the end of something

terrace: a wide, level step cut into the mountain side for growing crops. Farmers usually cut several terraces, one above the other

traditional: describes something that has been handed down from parents to their children for many years

transhumance: a method of farming in which animals are moved to fresh grass each season. The farmer may spend the summer high up on the mountain with the animals. In winter they are brought down to the lower slopes

tree line: the upper limit that trees will grow on a mountain

tropical: describes something to do with, or coming from, the tropics. The tropics are hot, damp parts of the world near the Equator

turbine: a wheel which has many curved blades. It is turned by water or gas. Turbines drive machines which make electricity

vent: an opening in the outer shell of the Earth that leads down into the melted rock beneath. A volcano forms around a vent

viaduct: a long, high bridge which carries a road or a railway across a valley

weathering: the action of weather on rock. Wind, ice, rain and heat wear away the surface of the rock, or break it up

Index